Can My Business Survive My Vacation?

A Practical Guide For Business Owners and Managers Who Dream of Taking A Vacation

Peter Biadasz and Mary Jo (MJ) Ross

Copyright 2023 Peter Biadasz and Mary Jo (MJ) Ross

All rights reserved.

No part of this book may be reproduced, stored in a
retrieval system, or transmitted by any means,
electronic, mechanical, photocopying, recording,
or otherwise, without written permission
from the author.

ISBN: 978-1-63302-267-6

What People Are Saying

"Peter and MJ have the experience, expertise, and have come up with the blueprint to keep things running smoothly while you are away because everyone needs and deserves to go on vacation or take some time off without worrying. This book is your key to stress free time off!"

Michelle Lee Myrter
Michelle Lee Business Coaching LLC
Certified B.A.N.K.™ Coach

"Whether your business has just a few associates, or many employees, Peter and MJ have developed a guide to enable you to relax on vacation without worry about what's happening back in the office; and to avoid returning to a disaster. It's well worth your time."

Rick Bahlinger
Runners Licensing, Inc.

"Just trying to identify all the things that need to be done to set my business up for success while I'm gone makes me want to creatively avoid the task. Peter and MJ have done all that thinking work for me. Thank you!"

Merianne Drew
Merianne Drew Coaching

"If you are looking for a book from business leaders who've already "succeeded in the trenches," you've arrived. This book is a great tool for the successful business owner who is ready for the next level. Don't let this title fool you into thinking this text is simply about business continuity during vacation. Yes, you'll have a great time away, but the secret sauce here is implementing the systems and the disciplines that set your business up for growth and long-term success. Bon voyage!"

Iris Culp
President, IC Growth
www.ic-growth.com
iris@ic-growth.com

"So many entrepreneurs put off enjoying life or even fear taking a vacation because they feel their business will fall apart if they leave for more than a few days. MJ and Peter teaming up on a project like this is a great idea! They both have amazing knowledge, skills, and experience. The information in this book will be incredibly useful to business owners wanting to gain peace of mind and prepare their business for long-term success."

Camille Diaz
Optimization Coach
The Optimized Zone

"Peter Biadasz is a prolific writer, accomplished publisher, and successful business owner. He and his writing partner on this book, MJ Ross, a savvy small business consultant, provide a deep dive into a topic rarely discussed, *Can My Business Survive My Vacation?* They cover a broad range of topics, in an "everything you need to know" book to ensure that you have a business to come back to after you take some much-needed time off. The chapters not only offer a detailed checklist of issues to consider, but they also offer best practices for sustaining any business in a healthy and intentional way. This is a clear and innovative help for small business owners."

Rena Cook, author and
founder of Vocal Authority

"I have known Mary Jo for over 20+ Years and I consider her a Business Mentor and friend. We share the same philosophy of life, which is to work hard but enjoy the time you worked so hard for.

She has deep and broad business leadership experience and is one of the most organized people I have worked with. She develops strong networks and as a result has built a successful consulting business and I love that she is passing along these pearls of wisdom."

Sherry Crowe
CEO, OncoConnects LLC

"I feel the workbook style is what is needed for today's busy business owner. The format allows the team to walk through important questions and understand the answers together. I was especially in need of, and grateful for, the section covering how to enjoy and get the most out of a well-earned vacation. Read this section twice.

The post-vacation, after-action portion at the end of the book was refreshingly new and missing from every other product in this space. I should mention that Mary Jo has worked with me and my business for many years now. My revenue has more than doubled, and I enjoy a long and rewarding vacation each year following these guidelines to the letter."

John L. Ross, Jr., CMRP
Maintenance Innovators, Inc.

Dedication

I dedicate this book to Mom and Dad; world travelers many times over and EXCELLENT examples of how to enjoy your vacation while watching your business grow. (Peter Biadasz)

I dedicate this book to my children and grandchildren. May you enjoy many travels and adventures without being tied down to your business. (Mary Jo Ross)

Table of Contents

Why Read This Book?..xiii

Acknowledgements...xv

Introduction..xvii

How this book is organized xix

Section 1

BEFORE your vacation:..1

1. Ensure all policies and procedures manuals
    are up to date 2
2. Set up systems, and document them......................3
3. Ensure all passwords are current, updated
    and protected while available to the
    right people 4
4. Prepare your business in advance for
    your vacation..5
5. Make sure any upcoming payroll issues will
    be handled appropriately before you leave 6

6. Document who will have the authority to access bank account info in your absence. Talk to your banker, attorney, CPA, etc....................7

7. Contact key clients as necessary............................8

8. Prepare and train your employees for your absence 9

9. Disaster recovery plan....................................... 10

10. Steps to take if any of the computers won't start in the morning, when to call in help, and whom to call... 11

11. IT Items include what to do if the internet connection goes down, router and cable modem locations — what to look for and how to reset them 12

12. Vendor lists and contact information (phone numbers, names of key contacts)............ 13

13. Company website troubleshooting if it goes down or appears to be down....................... 14

14. Social Media Items 15

15. Phone company contact person name, direct or cell number, email address..................... 16

16. Whom to call to deal with workspace/building maintenance (name, phone number) 17

17. Security company information and contact number plus passcode............................ 18

18. Ensure all insurance policies are current, appropriate and offer full coverage as needed... 19

19. Prioritize 20
20. If possible and practical, plan vacations
    around slow periods 21
21. Delegate 22
22. Define a clear Chain of Command 23
23. Prepare your employees/co-workers –
    and clearly identify who they will be
    reporting to in your absence 24
24. Designate a gatekeeper who will be the sole
    person who can determine what an emergency
    situation is that can't be handled and if and
    when you need to be contacted. Everything
    else can wait! 25
25. Calendar management 26
26. Set e-mail management expectations for
    during your vacation 27
27. Set protocols to delegate/forward your
    e-mail traffic 28
28. List all your emergency phone numbers and
    e-mail addresses, as well as the emergency
    contact information of those deemed as
    your significant others or family members 29

Section 2

DURING your vacation: 31

29. Set vacation rules for yourself 32
30. Enjoy your vacation 33
31. Check in only at prearranged times 34
32. Manage e-mails per the protocols set
    before your vacation 35
33. Unplug 36
34. Don't wear a watch unless you have to —
    no technology to cheat and check messages
    and emails 37
35. Sleep 38
36. Awareness of what you eat/drink 39

Section 3

AFTER your vacation: 41

37. Evaluate 42
38. Modify 44
39. Compliment 46
40. Check your calendar 47
41. Catch up 48
42. Plan your next vacation 49

Appendices 51

Index 55

About the Authors 57

Why Read This Book?

Are you delaying your vacation because you fear disaster will happen to your business, department or professional life when you are away? Or... do you take your "vacation" with phone, paperwork and ipad/laptop in hand, trying to do work and play simultaneously?

Vacations are important as they allow you to reset, unwind and offer a new perspective on your business. It also lets your teams show their worth/competence, etc. Your time away also confirms that you are hiring the types of employees who allow you to take vacations.

Can My Business Survive My Vacation? presents practical things you can do before, during and after your vacation to ensure a relaxing, refreshing time away from work while your business continues its day-to-day operations.

Acknowledgements

MUCH thanks to my family for being my earthly foundation, my friends for your acceptance and loyalty, my mentors for knowledge coupled with example, and my God for making all of this possible. It does take a team, and I am blessed with the best! (Peter Biadasz)

To my sons and my adopted family, thank you so much for your support and patience, and to God for being an important part of my life. To my mentors and friends, you have made a big difference! (Mary Jo Ross)

We both want to thank our weekly BAG (Business Advisory Group) members who offer encouragement, education, motivation, and accountability. This book is tangible proof of the effectiveness and importance of the group and the quality of its membership.

Introduction

~~~~~~~~~~~~~

You Need This Book If ...

You want a vacation

but are worried about what will happen to your
business while you are on vacation.

You need a vacation

and don't care what happens to your business when
you are on vacation.

You take work with you on vacation

and return more tired than when you
started your vacation.

You have not had a vacation in a while

and want to feel good about what is happening in your
business while you are on vacation.

You are a manager

and are afraid of what your employees will do when
you are on vacation.

You are a spouse or family member

who is tired of not being able to have a TRUE
vacation because the other person is tied up with work.

<u>You May Want To Gift This Book To ...</u>

Travel agents

People you know who love to travel

Dreamers who want to go on vacation

Workaholics

Entrepreneurs

Business owners

Franchisees

The most successful businessmen and women in your life

How this book is organized

This book is organized into 3 very distinct sections:

- **Before your vacation** is written in a fashion to ensure thoroughness with regards to all the areas to be addressed in detail before you leave for vacation.
- **During your vacation** lets you enjoy your vacation stress-free, to the fullest.
- **After your vacation** asks all the questions you may want to ponder as you feel not only rested from your adventures but confident in what your company accomplished in your absence.

Each section details items to be addressed and completed with blank lines added so you can customize each point to your situation.

<u>Section 1</u>

<u>BEFORE your vacation</u>

Much of this should have been done before you ever opened your business, but better late than never!

Note: If it makes you feel better, you can (and probably should) do a trial run for at least a couple of days if you've never taken a vacation from your business.

Can My Business Survive My Vacation?

1. **Ensure all policies and procedures manuals are up to date** – Be sure to include ALL steps involved in your processes and procedures. No detail is too small to document. To ensure your thoroughness have someone with no knowledge of a task perform the task as outlined in your manual. Do this exercise for all tasks addressed in your manuals. It will be quite clear if a step is not accurately documented.

   A. Have you developed company-wide policies? Are they documented?
   B. Have you made a list of all your departments?
   C. Have you listed all the tasks performed within each department?
   D. Have you written detailed instructions on how to perform each task?
   E. Have you backed up the documentation compiled in steps A – D?

Additional steps to consider and implement:

_____

_____

_____

_____

2. **Set up systems, and document them** – Be thorough in your setup and documentation.

   A. Have you set up systems or methodologies unique to your company?

   B. Have you thoroughly documented those systems?

   C. Have you backed up the documentation compiled in steps A & B?

Additional steps to consider and implement:

_____

_____

_____

_____

_____

_____

_____

_____

_____

_____

Can My Business Survive My Vacation?

3. **Ensure all passwords are current, updated and protected while available to the right people —** Document as hard copy and protected digital files.

   A. Does your IT Department have written protocols for password creation, modification and protection?
   B. Is there a secure list of passwords?
   C. Are all passwords current and updated?
   D. Are all passwords protected per company standards?
   E. Are all passwords backed up and secure?

Additional steps to consider and implement:

_____

_____

_____

_____

_____

_____

_____

_____

4. **Prepare your business in advance for your vacation** – Be sure to implement EVERY ITEM in this article.

    A. Does everyone in your company have a copy of this book?
    B. Has everyone in your company read this book?
    C. Have you met with management/supervisors to review this information and share expectations?
    D. Have management/supervisors met with their employees to review this material and share expectations?

Additional steps to consider and implement:

_____

_____

_____

_____

_____

_____

_____

_____

Can My Business Survive My Vacation?

5. **Make sure any upcoming payroll issues will be handled appropriately before you leave** – Be sure to include overtime and bonus pay as needed.

   A. Ensure all payroll policy and procedures manuals are current.
   B. Meet with those responsible for payroll processing to ensure there will be no payroll issues while you are gone.

Additional steps to consider and implement:

_____

_____

_____

_____

_____

_____

_____

_____

_____

_____

Peter Biadasz and Mary Jo (MJ) Ross

6. **Document who will have the authority to access bank account info in your absence. Talk to your banker, attorney, CPA, etc.** — Document, and communicate!

   A. List all bank accounts.
   B. Document the primary signers for each account.
   C. Document who are the secondary, and tertiary (if needed) signers on each account.
   D. Ensure your records and the bank records are in agreement.
   E. Discuss A – D above with your banker, attorney, CPA, etc., for additional recommendations or relevant information. Discuss best case/worst case scenarios with them.

Additional steps to consider and implement:

_____

_____

_____

_____

_____

_____

Can My Business Survive My Vacation?

7. **Contact key clients as necessary** – Ensure your customer base experiences no surprises in your absence.

   A. Create a list of your key clients.
   B. Develop a plan to communicate with those key clients significant things occurring within your company which may affect them.
   C. Implement the plan.
   D. Follow-up to ensure the plan was implemented properly and effectively.
   E. Modify the plan as needed.

Additional steps to consider and implement:

_____

_____

_____

_____

_____

_____

_____

_____

8. **Prepare and train your employees for your absence** — This may involve practicing and role-playing scenarios key to your business before you leave.

   A. Ensure all policies and procedures manuals are current and available to all employees as needed.
   B. Review the policies and procedures with all employees. Test employees if needed to feel comfortable with the competence levels.
   C. Detect weaknesses and address them accordingly. This may include retraining and role-play of trouble scenarios.
   D. Ensure each department has a backup plan.
   E. Ensure each employee is assigned someone in the event they need assistance of any type.

Additional steps to consider and implement:

_____

_____

_____

_____

_____

Can My Business Survive My Vacation?

9. **Disaster recovery plan** – Be sure to include OFF-SITE BACK-UP of everything!

   A. Develop and document a comprehensive Disaster Recovery Plan to ensure your business continues to operate effectively regardless of circumstances or lack of employee availability.
   B. Ensure management and employees have been trained on how to implement the Disaster Recovery Plan.
   C. To ensure B. talk through various scenarios, solicit responses, role play, etc.

Additional steps to consider and implement:

_____

_____

_____

_____

_____

_____

_____

Peter Biadasz and Mary Jo (MJ) Ross

10. **Steps to take if any of the computers won't start in the morning, when to call in help, and whom to call** – Document and communicate with all key individuals involved.

   A. Document step-by-step procedures to be followed when a computer will not start.
   B. Create a list of all IT personnel with contact information. Note that this list may differ from the IT internet personnel list in 11.B. below or the webmaster listed in 13.B. below.
   C. Ensure IT personnel assets are available 24/7/365 in the event of a catastrophic event, weather or otherwise.

Additional steps to consider and implement:

_____

_____

_____

_____

_____

_____

_____

_____

Can My Business Survive My Vacation?

11. **IT Items include what to do if the internet connection goes down, router and cable modem locations — what to look for and how to reset them —** Document and communicate with all key individuals involved.

   A. Document step-by-step procedures to be followed in the event of an internet outage.
   B. Create a list of all personnel involved in internet troubleshooting. Note this list may differ from the IT personnel list in 10. B. above or the webmaster noted in 13.B. below.
   C. Ensure internet-affiliated personnel assets are available 24/7/365 in the event of a catastrophic event, weather or otherwise.
   D. Create a list of all router and modem locations.
   E. Create a map of all internet cabling within your company.

Additional steps to consider and implement:

_____

_____

_____

_____

_____

Peter Biadasz and Mary Jo (MJ) Ross

12. **Vendor lists and contact information (phone numbers, names of key contacts)** — Ensure only key individuals in your organization have this vital information.

    A. Create a detailed vendor list. The list may be alphabetized by company name and categorized based on the products and services offered to your company.
    B. Ensure each entry in your vendor list includes not only key contacts and their contact information but, when possible, their backup personnel and their manager/supervisor information.
    C. Distribute the detailed vendor list to key appropriate individuals within your organization. Document who has the list. Notify these individuals that this is privileged information not to be shared with unauthorized personnel and that the list cannot be copied.

Additional steps to consider and implement:

_____

_____

_____

Can My Business Survive My Vacation?

13. **Company website troubleshooting if it goes down or appears to be down** – Set a clear process to troubleshoot and resolve this specific situation.

    A. Document detailed procedures in the event the company website goes down or gives the appearance it has gone down.
    B. Create a list of the webmaster and all associated website personnel. Note this list may differ from the IT personnel list in 10.B. above and the IT internet personnel list in 11.B. above.
    C. Ensure website–affiliated personnel assets are available 24/7/365 in the event of a catastrophic event, weather or otherwise.

Additional steps to consider and implement:

_____

_____

_____

_____

_____

_____

14. **Social Media Items** — Ensure your primary, secondary and tertiary target audiences not only hear and see you online, but you also hear and see them.

A. List all social media currently being utilized.
B. List all passwords as well as those authorized to utilize those passwords.
C. Create/implement/fine-tune the social media strategy.
D. Create procedures to ensure the social media strategy continues to be fully implemented and fine-tuned in your absence.

Additional steps to consider and implement:

_____

_____

_____

_____

_____

_____

_____

Can My Business Survive My Vacation?

15. **Phone company contact person name, direct or cell number, email address** — Ensure who is to make the contact and, just in case, who the backup may be.

   A. Create a list of all telephone phone company vendors — cell phones and hard-wired office telephone lines.
   B. Add to this list all contact information of the primary contacts as well as their backup and supervisors/managers.
   C. Create procedures to address the event of a telephone outage to ensure the smooth operation of the business.

Additional steps to consider and implement:

_____

_____

_____

_____

_____

_____

_____

16. **Whom to call to deal with workspace/building maintenance (name, phone number)** — Again, ensure who is to make the contact and, just in case, who the backup may be.

A. Whether you are leasing your space or own your building ensure the written documents of the transaction are copied with both copies safely stored. Give access to your lawyer, business partners and other key management as needed,

B. Create a list of all workspace/building maintenance companies/individuals with all contact information.

C. Assign personnel within your organization as primary and secondary contacts for your employees to contact regarding maintenance issues.

D. Inform your employees whom to contact to address maintenance issues.

Additional steps to consider and implement:

_____

_____

_____

Can My Business Survive My Vacation?

17. **Security company information and contact number plus passcode:** Again, ensure who is to make the contact and, just in case, who the backup may be.

   A. Create procedures to address the event of a security alarm being set off during non-business hours. This will include primary and secondary backup procedures in case of a break-in, fire, etc.
   B. Create a list of all security company vendors – cell phones and hard-wired office telephone lines.
   C. Add to the list in 16.B. above all contact information at those vendors of the primary contacts and their back-up and supervisors/managers.
   D. Create procedures to address the event of a security system outage to ensure the smooth operation of the business.
   E. Ensure you have local law enforcement and fire department contacts.

Additional steps to consider and implement:

_____

_____

_____

18. **Ensure all insurance policies are current, appropriate and offer full coverage as needed** — In the unfortunate case something minor or catastrophic happens to you have peace of mind all circumstances are safeguarded by the appropriate insurance policies.

   A. List all insurance policies, company and personal, currently in place. Include what is covered, time frames and the dollar values.
   B. Meet with your insurance agent(s) to determine if there are any gaps in your insurance to ensure that in the unfortunate case something minor or catastrophic happens to you or your company, business can proceed, or grow, in spite of any events or circumstances.

Additional steps to consider and implement:

_____

_____

_____

_____

_____

Can My Business Survive My Vacation?

19. **Prioritize** — Detail and customize for your situation, this can be a long and involved list.

   A. Create a detailed list of your company's priorities. List by as many categories and sub-categories as possible such as by division, department, function, customer, situation, weather, economic circumstances (both internal and external), personnel changes, etc. You can never be too creative with this list.
   B. Get input from many trusted individuals inside and outside your company to ensure thoroughness.
   C. Once the priority list is complete by category, prioritize each category's items.
   D. Ensure each person/department/etc. is informed of the list along with understanding how they and their function fit into it, and thereby the company as a whole.

Additional steps to consider and implement:

_____

_____

_____

_____

20. **If possible and practical, plan vacations around slow periods** – Clearly understand your yearly business cycle.

   A. Create charts showing your sales over the past 3 – 5 years.
   B. Note the slowest and busiest times.
   C. While you can plan a vacation around slow periods, create a plan to create more business during these periods, thus eliminating your slowest times of the year.
   D. When C. is achieved, groom someone you can delegate to when you take your well-deserved vacation.

Additional steps to consider and implement:

_____

_____

_____

_____

_____

_____

Can My Business Survive My Vacation?

21. **Delegate** – Hire and train so you can delegate with MUCH confidence.

    A. Perform a detailed examination of your hiring practices and training programs.
    B. Address any deficiencies and strengthen the areas already doing well.
    C. Create a program to cross-train employees on related functions.
    D. Determine via testing and role-playing at what point someone is cross- trained to the point of efficiently and accurately performing multiple functions.
    E. Recognize and compensate accordingly.

Additional steps to consider and implement:

_____

_____

_____

_____

_____

_____

_____

22. **Define a clear Chain of Command** – make sure that the person you are leaving in charge is aware of that and has accepted the responsibility.

A. Create an organizational chart of your company, both high-level and detailed.
B. Ensure there exists a detailed job description for each position.
C. Not only publish the organizational chart internally but ensure each manager/supervisor meets with their staff to clearly explain the chart.
D. Include the organizational chart in every new employee hire packet/orientation.
E. Update the organization chart as needed.
F. Review the organizational chart in detail on a yearly basis to ensure all information listed is current.

Additional steps to consider and implement:

_____

_____

_____

_____

_____

Can My Business Survive My Vacation?

23. **Prepare your employees/co-workers — and clearly identify who they will be reporting to in your absence —** Create an organizational chart to ensure there are no misunderstandings regarding the chain of command.

A. See 21.
B. Hold meeting(s) before you leave on vacation to ensure there are no misunderstandings or misinterpretations of the organizational chart in your absence.

Additional steps to consider and implement:

_____

_____

_____

_____

_____

_____

_____

_____

_____

Peter Biadasz and Mary Jo (MJ) Ross

24. **Designate a gatekeeper who will be the sole person who can determine what an emergency situation is that can't be handled and if and when you need to be contacted. Everything else can wait!** — Your most trusted and experienced employee.

    A. Make a list of your 3 most reliable, experienced, informed and trusted employees.
    B. To avoid confusion rank them in order (primary, secondary, tertiary).
    C. Inform the 3 they are on this list as well as their ranking order.
    D. Make a list of situations and circumstances in which you must be contacted. Ensure these are life/death scenarios for your business or those involved. Understand it will be hard to let go of some items and delegate in your absence.
    E. Review the list made in D. in detail with the 3 on your trusted list. Ensure they understand what constitutes a true emergency.
    F. Give all 3 individuals your "on-vacation contact information." Inform them they are NOT to share this information with anyone!

Additional steps to consider and implement:

_____

_____

_____

Can My Business Survive My Vacation?

25. **Calendar management** — To ensure everything is accomplished on time.

   A. Review your calendar to ensure it is current 30 days before you leave for vacation.
   B. Complete all tasks/ appointments/etc. as much as possible before you leave for vacation.
   C. Delegate what is left to be completed.
   D. Designate 1 person to schedule appointments for you while you are gone. Ensure that person gives you details for each appointment.

Additional steps to consider and implement:

_____

_____

_____

_____

_____

_____

_____

_____

Peter Biadasz and Mary Jo (MJ) Ross

26. **Set e-mail management expectations for during your vacation** – Delegate as much as you reasonably can.

    A. Make a list of customers and situations which may need attention while you are on vacation.
    B. Meet with your staff to discuss and document a plan of action in the event the customers or situations need attention during your vacation.
    C. Set criteria for contacting you during your vacation due to an emergency e-mail situation.

Additional steps to consider and implement:

_____

_____

_____

_____

_____

_____

_____

_____

Can My Business Survive My Vacation?

27. **Set protocols to delegate/forward your e-mail traffic** — Create criteria to ensure e-mails are forwarded appropriately to the right people.

    A. In conjunction with 25. above, grant access to your e-mail to 1 trusted person, as well as a backup in case your #1 is sick, etc.

    B. Set a schedule for your e-mail to be checked.

    C. Set criteria for how an e-mail will be dispositioned — trash, address when you return or address right away and delegate.

    D. Set systems to guarantee any delegated e-mail is addressed and does not "fall through the cracks."

    E. Ensure everyone involved in 25 and 26 is confident in your expectations regarding handling your e-mails in your absence.

Additional steps to consider and implement:

_____

_____

_____

_____

_____

Peter Biadasz and Mary Jo (MJ) Ross

28. **List all your emergency phone numbers and e-mail addresses, as well as the emergency contact information of those deemed as your significant others or family members.**

    A. Make a list of any who would be deemed as a significant other or family member you would want to be contacted in the event you are sick, injured or die while on vacation.
    B. List the contact information for everyone on the list.
    C. Ensure your emergency gatekeeper and another trusted individual in your company have a copy of this list.
    D. Make a list of all of your e-mail passwords. Share in a sealed envelope only with your emergency gatekeeper and another trusted individual with instructions that the envelope can only be opened under catastrophic circumstances.

Additional steps to consider and implement:

_____

_____

_____

Section 2

DURING your vacation

What is your goal? Rest? Or something else?

Can My Business Survive My Vacation?

29. **Set vacation rules for yourself** – Follow your self-created rules with a smile!

    A. Is one of them to have fun?
    B. Do you have detailed plans for everything you want to accomplish during your vacation?
    C. Or do you prefer to relax and play it by ear?
    D. Are your rules made just by you or in conjunction with whomever you are traveling with?
    E. Can you avoid setting an alarm?
    F. Is a daily nap included in your rules?
    G. What is your end goal?
        1. Relaxed, refreshed, and have more energy?
        2. Exhausted, you say, "I need a vacation from my vacation."

If the latter is true, you might not have read this book thoroughly.

Additional steps to consider and implement:

_____

_____

_____

_____

_____

30. **Enjoy your vacation** — After all, it is YOUR vacation!

   A. Do you plan to check out new restaurants or new types of food?
   B. Are you going to try something new such as an excursion?
   C. Do you have sunscreen and the appropriate gear? Or can you rent or buy it?
   D. Is everything a group decision, or do different people get to select different activities?
   E. Is any spa time involved?
   F. What can the person who uses their phone only for pictures (stays in airplane mode) get as a reward?

Additional steps to consider and implement:

_____

_____

_____

_____

_____

_____

Can My Business Survive My Vacation?

31. **Check in only at prearranged times** – Maintain a schedule to protect your relaxation time.

   A. If you must check in on family, pets, or anyone else, is it possible to do so only twice a day (preferably only once) during a set time?
   B. How addicted are you to work?
   C. How many more hours do you have in your day when you follow this protocol?
   D. How does one-on-one time feel when you aren't distracted and can be fully present?

Additional steps to consider and implement:

_____

_____

_____

_____

_____

_____

_____

_____

_____

Peter Biadasz and Mary Jo (MJ) Ross

32. **Manage e-mails per the protocols set before your vacation** — Relax, delegate, repeat ...

   A. Remember you have people trained to handle things for you, including forwarding e-mails to the appropriate person to take care of, so you can enjoy your vacation.
   B. One person should be letting you know what something is you absolutely must manage. If the e-mail is not from that person, please ignore it.

Additional steps to consider and implement:

_____

_____

_____

_____

_____

_____

_____

_____

Can My Business Survive My Vacation?

33. **Unplug** – Ensure you have time alone, or with loved ones, with NO technology.

   A. If it will help, have a contest to see who can go without technology the longest.
   B. Even if it is awkward at first, enjoy that one-on-one time.
   C. If the weather doesn't cooperate, play board or card games.
   D. Leave your laptop or iPad in the safe or at least out of sight except for prearranged times.
   E. Can you keep your smartphone in airplane mode so you can take pictures but avoid contacting anyone or sneaking online?

Additional steps to consider and implement:

_____

_____

_____

_____

_____

_____

_____

Peter Biadasz and Mary Jo (MJ) Ross

34. **Don't wear a watch unless you have to — no technology to cheat and check messages and e-mails — A naked wrist is a happy wrist!**

    A. Leave your watch in the safe so you won't keep looking at it.
    B. If you must have a watch, take an analog one.

Additional steps to consider and implement:

_____

_____

_____

_____

_____

_____

_____

_____

_____

_____

_____

Can My Business Survive My Vacation?

35. **Sleep** – Get caught up on lost sleep, nap as you want, and recharge yourself.

A. Zzzzzzzz.
B. Rest your eyes if you can't sleep
C. Don't forget to pack earplugs if you need them.

Additional steps to consider and implement:

36. **Awareness of what you eat/drink** – Ensure you eat/drink, for the most part, what will be best for your short and long-term health.

   A. Know what kinds of transportation are available and how to contact them so you can get back to your location safely.
   B. Ask the hotel or resort staff (or someone you know who is familiar with the area) for recommendations for food/drink and safety.
   C. Follow basic safety protocols when purchasing drinks and protecting them.

Additional steps to consider and implement:

_____

_____

_____

_____

_____

_____

_____

_____

Section 3

AFTER your vacation

Enjoy your travels, knowing your business WILL survive your vacation!

Can My Business Survive My Vacation?

37. **Evaluate** – Examine each detail of this list to understand what worked and what did not.

   A. Did you have to put out any fires while on vacation?
   B. Are there any fires you need to address immediately, or can someone else handle them?
   C. Was your gatekeeper able to keep things under control, so you were only bothered by an emergency or a critical situation?
   D. Did any of your staff skip the gatekeeper and contact you directly?
   E. Were your designated e-mail checking times the only times you checked it?
   F. How many work calls or texts did you get from your gatekeeper while you were gone?
   G. How many work calls or texts did you make because you were worried about how things were going?
   H. How many phone messages and e-mails were waiting for you to handle that someone else could have taken care of?
   I. Are all your clients still your clients?
   J. Were there staff conflicts you needed to address?
   K. Is there much tension in the workplace, or is it relaxed and "business as usual?"

L. Did your staff achieve their predetermined goals during your time away? If not, why not? Were there circumstances beyond their control?

M. Did the person who monitored your email delegate to the appropriate people? Was there follow-through and follow-up by those staff people?

N. Were bills paid, invoiced, and deposited appropriately?

O. Was payroll handled smoothly (if applicable)?

P. Did you have a group conversation to process how it went?

Q. Did you talk to people individually, or have the appropriate supervisor or manager do so if appropriate?

R. Was the Chain of Command followed?

S. How do you feel after being gone and leaving everything to your staff?

T. Was it smooth sailing when you got home?

Additional steps to consider and implement:

Can My Business Survive My Vacation?

38. **Modify** — Modify the policies, procedures, documents, etc., as needed after your evaluation.

  A. Did things go smoothly? If not, was it a process issue, a personnel issue, or hadn't been addressed before your time away?
  B. What went well?
  C. What area(s) had issues?
  D. Were there any gaps that hadn't been anticipated?
  E. Any critical situations to review and establish how to address for the future?
  F. If there were computer issues, were they handled, or are they still an issue?
  G. Any security issues? If so, how do they need to be addressed?
  H. Were there any issues with social media?
  I. If so, were they violations of your social media policies and procedures?
  J. Did only the designated staff person manage all social media in your absence?
  K. Are there any personnel issues left for you to deal with?
  L. Was there anyone who took advantage of your absence to avoid their job?
  M. Was there a conflict with your designated representative and others who refused to cooperate?

N. Do you think additional training should exist for certain areas or people? If so, discover why and involve the appropriate team members to solve gaps or issues.

O. Is everything in place for you to go on another vacation?

P. Are there plans to ensure your staff gets their vacation time and is covered while they are gone?

Additional steps to consider and implement:

_____

_____

_____

_____

_____

_____

_____

_____

_____

_____

Can My Business Survive My Vacation?

39. **Compliment** – Let your team know what they did right to ensure the positive health of the company while you were gone.

  A. Thank them for keeping things running smoothly and giving you real vacation time (group praise).
  B. Make sure and take the time to personally thank them on an individual basis.
  C. Is there a way to reward them for it going well? (company lunch, event, gift cards, etc.)
  D. Were there certain people who stepped up to the plate?
  E. How can you recognize them so you are focusing on the positive instead of anything negative that may have taken place?
  F. Were there any people who joined the team while you were gone to ensure things ran smoothly? (can include volunteers, spouses, etc.)

Additional steps to consider and implement:

_____

_____

_____

Peter Biadasz and Mary Jo (MJ) Ross

40. **Check your calendar** — Ensure you did not miss anything while away.

   A. Did you block at least two days on your calendar after your return so you can catch up without clients or other meetings you need to prepare for?
   B. Were there any missed deadlines?
   C. How could the missed deadlines have been avoided?
   D. What upcoming deadlines do you have?
   E. Can someone else take responsibility for an upcoming deadline?
   F. Have additional events or appointments been added to your calendar since you left?
   G. Can the events or appointments be delegated, or are they most appropriate for you to handle?
   H. If you have tentative plans for your next vacation, block that time now. It can always change.

Additional steps to consider and implement:

_____

_____

_____

Can My Business Survive My Vacation?

41. **Catch up** – Set a timeline to catch up quickly and thoroughly.

    A. Did you ask your gatekeeper or manager to provide a written summary for you to read the evening before or the morning of your first day back?
    B. Do you have a time scheduled to meet with your staff as a group to debrief about your absence?
    C. What is the best way for staff to suggest changes or improvements for the time during your next vacation?
    D. How can you ensure the verbal and other feedback you get is implemented into your new vacation plan, policies, and procedures?
    E. Blocking at least two days after your return to get caught up will help you be in the correct mindset to transition back into your regular schedule.

Additional steps to consider and implement:

_____

_____

_____

42. **Plan your next vacation** – Your next vacation will be more fun, having already followed these guidelines for your last vacation.

   A. Are you ready for a more extended vacation?
   B. Was the one you went on too long or too short?
   C. Where are you going next time?
   D. How often will you build your vacation time into your annual schedule moving forward?
   E. How soon can you confirm the details with your travel agent or whoever schedules your trips?

Additional steps to consider and implement:

_____

_____

_____

_____

_____

_____

_____

_____

_____

_____

Can My Business Survive My Vacation?

Now that you have peace of mind and a plan, where do you want to go for your next vacation?

_____

_____

_____

Future vacation destinations:

_____

_____

_____

Enjoy your travels, knowing your business WILL survive your vacation.

Appendices

Can My Business Survive My Vacation?

Can My Business Survive My Vacation?

CHECKLIST

By Peter Biadasz — Author, Speaker, Publisher, Consultant
And Mary Jo (MJ) Ross - Small Business Consultant

BEFORE your vacation:

- Update policies and procedures manuals
- Set up and document those systems
- Address passwords
- Prepare your business in advance for your vacation
- Address payroll
- Address bank account info
- Contact key clients
- Prepare and train your employees for your absence
- Disaster recovery plan
- Address computer restarts
- IT Items
- Vendor lists/contact information
- Website troubleshooting
- Social Media
- Internet items
- Phone company contact
- Workspace/building maintenance
- Security company information
- Insurance Policies
- Prioritize
- Plan vacations around slow periods
- Delegate
- Define a clear Chain of Command
- Prepare your employees/ co-workers
- Designate a gatekeeper
- Calendar management
- E-mail management expectations
- Delegate/forward your e-mail traffic
- List all emergency contacts

DURING your vacation:

- Set your vacation goals
- Set vacation rules for yourself
- Enjoy your vacation
- Check in only at prearranged times
- Manage e-mails
- Unplug
- Don't wear a watch
- Sleep
- Awareness of what you eat/drink

AFTER your vacation:

- Evaluate
- Modify
- Compliment
- Check your calendar
- Catch up
- Plan your next vacation

Enjoy your travels, knowing your business WILL survive your vacation!

From the book
Can My Business Survive My Vacation?
Peter Biadasz — Author, Speaker, Publisher, Consultant And
MJ Ross — Small Business Consultant
Copyright 2022 Peter Biadasz and Mary Jo (MJ) Ross

Index

Bank account 7, 52

Business Cycles 21, 52

Calendar 26, 52

Calendar management 26, 52

Catch up 47, 48

Chain of Command 23, 52

Check in 34, 53

Clients, Key 8, 52

Compliment 46, 53

Computer 11, 44, 52

Contact key clients 8, 52

Delegate 21, 22, 25, 28, 35, 43, 52

Disaster recovery plan 10, 52

Document those systems 3, 52

Eat/drink 39, 53

E-mail 27, 28, 29, 35, 52

E-mail traffic 28, 52

Emergency contacts 24, 52

Enjoy 33, 41, 50, 53, 56

Can My Business Survive My Vacation?

Evaluate 42, 44, 53

Gatekeeper 25, 29, 42, 48, 52

Goals 42, 53

Insurance Policies 19, 52

Internet items 52

IT Items 12, 52

Next vacation 47, 48, 49, 50, 53

Organizational Chart 24, 52

Passwords 4, 15, 29, 52

Payroll 6, 43, 52

Phone company contact 16, 52

Policies and procedures manuals 2, 9, 52

Prepare 5, 9, 24, 52

Prioritize 20, 52

Security company information 18, 52

Sleep 38, 53

Slow periods 21, 52

Social Media 15, 52

Train 9, 22, 52

Unplug 36, 53

Vacation rules 32, 53

Vendor lists 13, 52

Watch 37, 53

Website 14, 52

Workspace/building maintenance 17, 52

About the Authors

Peter Biadasz, President of Total Publishing And Media, has authored/co-authored 18 books including "Write Your First Book," now in its 2nd edition and "More Leads," a handbook for networkers. He is also a very active public speaker. His areas of expertise include Applied Mathematics and Theoretical Physics, as well as a degree in Psychology, aiding him to build bridges between the often-diverse worlds of social and natural sciences. Enjoy Peter's Video Shorts on YouTube and Facebook. Feel free to contact Peter at peter@TotalPublishingAndMedia.com

MJ Ross, President of MJ Executive Consulting, LLC, focuses on helping small business owners "future proof" with business continuity planning, including pre-vacation, succession and exit planning. She previously edited "Strategies," an oncology digital monthly magazine for two years. She was executive director for 6 nonprofit oncology state associations at the same

Can My Business Survive My Vacation?

time for 14 years and helped pass 7 laws benefiting cancer patients. During that time, she also owned an association management business for 10 years where she hadn't known to do the "future proofing" so she was unable to sell her business when she wanted to, and instead, had to close it down. Feel free to contact her at mjross@mjexecconsulting.com

Printed in the USA
CPSIA information can be obtained
at www.ICGtesting.com
LVHW021359051023
760085LV00064B/2187